Sea Monsters

Ancient Reptiles That Ruled the Sea

Written by David Eldridge
Illustrated by Norman Nodel

Troll Associates

Pronunciation Guide

Archelon	(AR-kuh-lon)
Brontosaurus	(Bron-tuh-SAWR-us)
Elasmosaurus	(Ee-laz-muh-SAWR-us)
Hesperornis	(Hes-per-OR-niss)
ichthyosaur	(IK-thee-uh-sawr)
Ichthyosaurus	(Ik-thee-uh-SAWR-us)
Kronosaurus	(Kron-uh-SAWR-us)
Mesosaurus	(Mez-uh-SAWR-us)
mosasaurs	(MO-zuh-sawrz)
Nothosaurus	(No-tho-SAWR-us)
Placodus	(PLAK-uh-dus)
plesiosaur	(PLEEZ-ee-uh-sawr)
Plesiosaurus	(Pleez-ee-uh-SAWR-us)
Trachodon	(TRAK-uh-don)
Trinacomerium	(Trih-nih-ko-MEER-ee-um)
Tylosaurus	(Tie-luh-SAWR-us)

During the great Age of Dinosaurs, the world was far different from the world of today. The air was warm and moist. Most of the land was swampy. Giant ferns, shrubs, and palm-like trees grew everywhere. Dinosaurs ruled the land, and flying reptiles ruled the air.

The seas were warm and shallow, and they covered many parts of the earth. Swimming and diving and leaping in these prehistoric seas were giant creatures. These "sea monsters" were really *reptiles* that lived in the water. Giant reptiles—like the ichthyosaurs — ruled the seas.

We know about the ichthyosaurs from fossils. Fossils are the remains of plants and animals that lived millions of years ago. A 12-year-old girl discovered the first fossil of an ichthyosaur in 1811. Trapped in the rock was a complete skeleton of a fish-like monster. What kind of creature was it?

Scientists who came to see the fossil skeleton were puzzled. It looked like the remains of a giant fish. It had paddles, or flippers, and a large fin on its back. But in other ways, the creature did not look like a fish at all. It had long, pointed jaws filled with teeth. Perhaps it was an ancient reptile.

Fish or reptile? Scientists decided to name the fossil Ichthyosaurus, or "fish-reptile." It was definitely a reptile, although it looked very much like a fish. Here was the fossil skeleton of a giant sea reptile that lived many millions of years ago. It had lived at the time when dinosaurs walked the earth.

The first animals on earth lived in the prehistoric seas. Slowly, some of the animals changed. They learned to live on the land. Then came the first reptiles. As millions of years went by, some of the reptiles changed again. Some became better suited to life in the sea. So they returned to the prehistoric oceans.

When these reptiles went back to the sea, their bodies became more and more fish-like. Their legs turned into paddle-like flippers, so they could swim faster. Some grew fins. But they did not have gills. The sea reptiles had to come to the surface to breathe air into their lungs.

Many of the sea-going reptiles grew to a great size. A few were almost as long as Brontosaurus, one of the largest dinosaurs. Some, like the ichthyosaurs, looked like monstrous fish. Others looked like weird sea serpents, or sea dragons. Still others looked like animals we know today, such as crocodiles and turtles.

Some sea reptiles left the water to lay their eggs on land. Others had to stay in the water all the time. Their eggs hatched inside the body of the mother, and the babies were born alive.

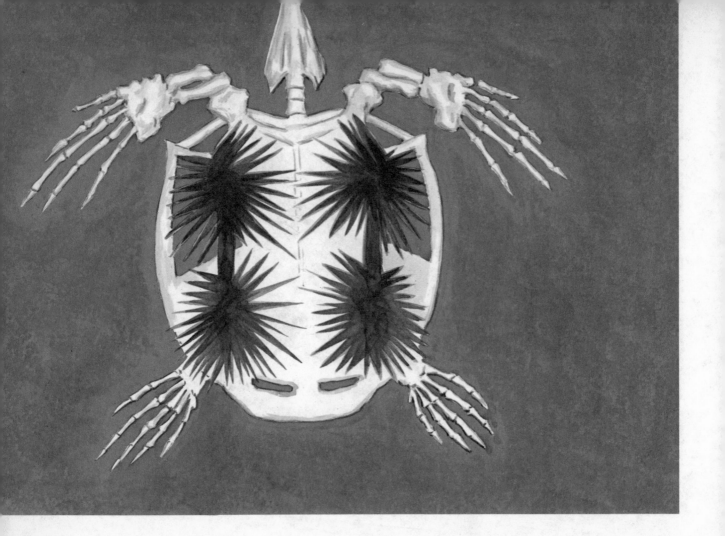

Swimming about in these ancient seas was the biggest turtle that ever lived. It was called Archelon, or "ruler turtle." Archelon was the prehistoric ancestor of today's much smaller turtles. But it did not have a hard shell covering its body. Instead, its bones formed a framework that did not weigh as much as a solid shell.

But Archelon was still very heavy. It was so heavy, that on land its legs were not strong enough to lift its huge body. To lay its eggs on the beach, it must have swum in with the rising tide. Then it had to wait for the next high tide, so it could return to the sea.

Prehistoric crocodiles were far larger than modern crocodiles. Some were over 50 feet long. Lying like a dead log in an ancient swamp, this huge reptile waited until an unsuspecting dinosaur came near. One blow from its great tail could stun a huge plant-eater like Trachodon. Then the crocodile's jaws finished the job.

One of the first reptiles to go back to the sea was Mesosaurus. It had a flat tail like an eel. It had webbed feet like a frog, and long, thin jaws like a crocodile. Mesosaurus had no trouble catching fish with its dagger-like teeth.

Nothosaurus was an early reptile that was at home on land or in the water. It grew as large as 10 feet long. In the water, it stretched its long neck out, and caught fish with its sharp teeth. It laid its eggs on land, and often just basked in the sun. Some scientists think that is why this strange creature died out. It may have spent so much time on land that meat-eating dinosaurs could easily catch it.

Later, there was another strange sea creature — called Placodus. It was about 5 feet long, and had a bullet-shaped head, short neck, and stubby flippers. But instead of sharp, fish-catching teeth, Placodus had blunt front teeth that jutted out of its mouth. As it swam along the sea bottom, Placodus used its teeth to tear snails and other shellfish loose from rocks.

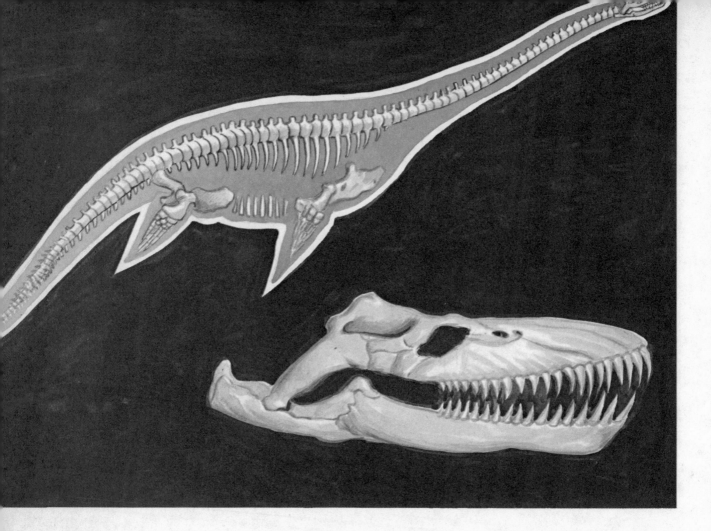

The same young girl who discovered the first skeleton of an ichthyosaur also found many other fossils. She later found a strange skeleton that was 10 feet long, and in perfect condition. It turned out to be one of the first complete fossils of a young Plesiosaurus.

For millions of years, gigantic plesiosaurs of all kinds swam through the warm prehistoric oceans. Some were as large as 50 feet in length. A typical plesiosaur had a saucer-shaped body with a long, snake-like neck at one end, and a long, thin tail at the other. The tiny head was filled with sharp teeth. Some plesiosaurs had a rudder-like fin on the tail.

As time went on, one kind of plesiosaur kept growing a longer and longer neck. This was Elasmosaurus. It may have reached a total length of 60 feet — about the same length as the great dinosaur, Brontosaurus. Elasmosaurus ate practically anything it could catch. Sometimes it caught Hesperornis, a diving bird that had teeth.

A sea monster the size of Elasmosaurus, with its long neck and four narrow flippers, was not built for speed. It may have paddled around slowly on top of the water looking for something to eat. Some scientists think it may have been able to "row" backwards as well as forwards.

Elasmosaurus would quietly paddle toward its prey. Then it would lash out its tiny head with lightning speed. With its long flexible neck, it could reach a large fish that was 20 feet away. Its sharp teeth were perfect for holding the slippery fish that made up the main part of its diet.

Other kinds of plesiosaurs *were* built for speed. One of these was Trinacomerium. This big reptile had a short neck, large head, and huge flippers. With a sudden burst of speed, it could slice through the water and attack its prey. Always hungry, this huge reptile could bite through the backbone of a large fish, or swallow it whole!

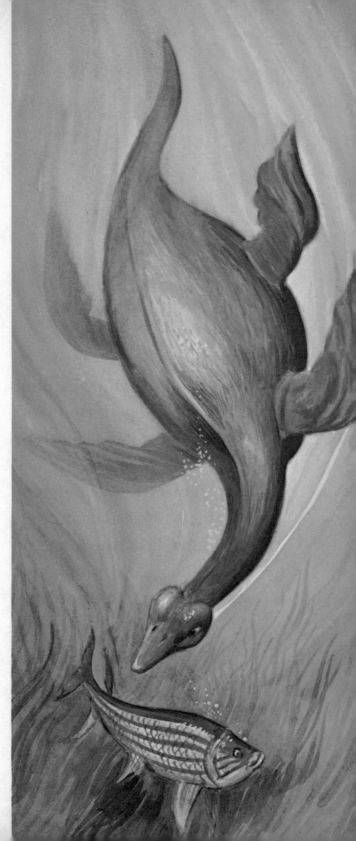

The biggest sea reptile of them all was called Kronosaurus. This whale-sized monster grew to a length of 55 feet. Its head was 13 feet long. Seizing large sea reptiles in its 8-foot-long jaws, it must have been the terror of the oceans. And any dinosaur that came too far into the water could be easily torn to pieces.

During the millions of years that the plesiosaurs lived, the ichthyosaurs also swam the seas. There were several members of this family of sea-going reptiles. Some were as small as 3 feet, while others reached lengths of 30 or 40 feet. The earliest kinds looked something like eels with long jaws. But later ichthyosaurs were shaped more like modern dolphins or porpoises.

Like today's dolphins, these ichthyosaurs were fast, powerful swimmers. An ichthyosaur swam simply by moving its body and tail from side to side like a fish. It could dart into a school of fish, slashing and biting with its long, toothed jaws. Then, when the school had scattered, the hungry reptile could take its time eating its victims.

Like all reptiles, the ichthyosaurs had lungs instead of gills. They could not breathe underwater, and would drown if they stayed below the surface too long. Even baby ichthyosaurs had to come to the surface before they could take their first breath of air.

Later, fierce reptiles called mosasaurs appeared in the prehistoric seas. Many fossils of these huge creatures have been found in the western United States. In ancient times, the broad sea that covered this area must have been alive with mosasaurs. Some were larger than many land reptiles, reaching a length of 40 feet.

Tylosaurus was one of the biggest and fiercest of the mosasaurs. One skeleton was nearly 50 feet long. Tylosaurus shot through the water by moving its long, flat tail back and forth. With its gigantic jaws, it could seize any fish or reptile that swam. In a few minutes, Tylosaurus could kill and eat a fish that weighed as much as 600 pounds.

Quite often, two great sea monsters of prehistoric times probably met and fought. Perhaps Elasmosaurus strayed into the favorite fishing waters of Tylosaurus. Or, perhaps one had a large fish that the other wanted. Suddenly, the two angry reptiles would snap and slash at each other. As they struggled, their thrashing bodies must have whipped the sea into white foam.

Elasmosaurus and Tylosaurus were among the last of the giant reptiles to rule the earth's ancient seas. They mysteriously died out about 70 million years ago. So did the mighty dinosaurs that ruled the land. And so did the huge flying reptiles that ruled the skies. Scientists are not sure exactly why this happened. One reason was probably a rapid cooling of the earth's climate.

The story of prehistoric animals never ends. A new chapter is written each time a new fossil skeleton is discovered. Scientists are especially interested in finding out more about the ancient sea reptiles. For a challenging mystery still remains about these mighty creatures of the prehistoric seas.